THE TWIN TOWERS

THE TWIN

TOWERS

AN ELEGY ▪ 1972-2001

FOREWORD BY MARLA HAMBURG KENNEDY

INTRODUCTION BY VICKI GOLDBERG

EDITED BY KELLY PADDEN

PUBLISHED BY PICTURE THIS PUBLICATIONS,

IN ASSOCIATION WITH

KENNEDY BOESKY PHOTOGRAPHS,

NEW YORK

TITLE PAGE: BURT GLINN

Publisher: Marla Hamburg Kennedy. Editor: Kelly Padden. Editorial Assistants: Amalia Culp and Tal Schpantzer. Design: Louise Fili Ltd. Copy Editor: Steve Hamburg. Picture This Publications and Kennedy Boesky Photographs 535 West 22nd Street, New York, NY 10011 Telephone 212.741.0963 Printed by the Stinehour Press, Lunenburg, Vermont. All proceeds will be donated to the Shainwald Charitable Foundation which will distribute monies to humanitarian organizations; Amnesty International and Médecins Sans Frontières (Doctors Without Borders). The publishers would like to thank all those who have made this project possible, including all the photographers, Magnum Photos, and Getty Images for donating the images, The Stinehour Press for printing, and Louise Fili Ltd for graphic design. ISBN# 0-9703983-2-8

FOREWORD

I CAME OF AGE IN NEW YORK CITY DURING THE TIME THE TWIN TOWERS WERE BUILT.
Even back then, their presence became a kind of compass for me, providing a unique sense of time, space, and place. For me, and for countless others like me, they will always represent a distinct era in the long history of the world's greatest metropolis. I feel honored to have had the Twin Towers as a part of my life.

Although it's never been fashionable to say so, I admired the Twin Towers architecturally. With their gothic stylizations, soaring height, and ethereal sense of weightlessness even in the face of such mass, they were our latter-day "Cathedrals of Commerce." Indeed, like medieval cathedrals, the Twin Towers embodied the intersection of art and technology. They took primitive, geometric forms (think Stonehenge) and transmuted them, through the language of steel and glass, into quintessential statements of the modern age.

We thought they were omnipotent. They hovered over us in a familial way. They seemed to protect us with their masculine strength. We could depend on them. They would never leave us, or worse, collapse on us. They would survive.

Their demise has left a spatial void in the heart of the city and, yes, a kind of spiritual void in our hearts. Their loss has reminded us of that most primary of lessons: that all material things will perish. With that in mind, we have no place to go but inward—and upward—again.   *Marla Hamburg Kennedy, October 2001*

I NEVER LIKED THE WORLD TRADE CENTER TOWERS. ARCHITECTURALLY, THEY WERE mediocre at best. Even as an emblem they were not beautiful, and height alone, I think, is not a flawless achievement—the hundredth floor takes a long time to get to, and once there, you feel very cut off from earth, from home.

Yet today I mourn the towers unconditionally and without stint. The appalling number of lives, mostly young lives, that were cut off in a wink of time would be far more than enough. Then there's the sense of freedom and security that I grew up with and that has disappeared into an intractable pile of rubble. The towers, symbol of finance and power and New York's mighty centrality, have mutated into a symbol of overwhelming darkness.

And then I find myself mourning the buildings themselves, with what strikes me as the kind of pain that might follow the death of parents you didn't get along with all that well. Their absolute disappearance suddenly makes it clear how invaluable they were after all, how irreplaceable, and how implacably their presence had shaped your personal view of the world you inhabit. The towers were a vital, instantly recognizable part of the New York skyline, that outline of an ambitious, braggart, technologically and culturally sophisticated Oz, where hearts and brains and bravery (and humbug too) were always in abundant supply.

The photographers on these pages liked the Center, or at least respected it, a good deal more than I did. (I don't know how they felt about it aesthetically; an object obviously doesn't have to be beautiful to be a splendid photographic subject or to be raised up to beauty bestowed on it by photographic ingenuity.) Through the eyes of these men and women the buildings attained what I was reluctant to see in them—a kind of majesty, an occasional dusting of glamour and romance—plus what we would all agree on, a sure stamp of inevitability, of unbreakable ties to the city. Events have fractured those ties, but not as successfully as they fractured the towers themselves.

Since September 11 the two skyscrapers have made a strange progress from monoliths of durable material to a ghostly efflorescence of images. Once celebrated, they have become celebrities. First there were the endless pictures of their death throes on TV. Then people raced to buy photographs, drawings, T-shirts, postcards, anything blazoned with those twin forms standing tall.

This is the afterlife that photography has conferred on celebrity. When Victoria's consort, Prince Albert, died in 1861, British subjects bought 70,000 copies of his portrait within a week. There are no figures for September, 2001, in New York, but for well over a month, every sidewalk where people peddled photographs offered more views of the towers dominating downtown, the towers with the Statue of Liberty, the towers at night, the towers up close or from a distance, than people who worked in them had ever had in one day. It was almost painful, seeing the lost buildings so often, like hearing a eulogy too many times.

Well, photography, which has been associated with death and loss from its inception, has been the sole commemoration for buildings before, much as it has been for people. Even in New York, a great building like Penn Station that we tore down ourselves only exists in photographs and a few memories today. In Germany after World War II, several cities were rebuilt exactly as they had been centuries before with the aid of old photographs.

Photography keeps being superceded by other visual forms—film, television, video, digital pastiche—but it turns around again and again to prove itself urgent. Where would memory be without it? When photographs of the towers sprang up in stores and on the sidewalks, that was for economic reasons, sure, but everyone knew how circumstances had changed the meaning and significance of these pictures that were once simpler in intent. Famous photographers culled their files for images to donate to the cause. Professional and amateur photographs of the disaster joined together in a monumentally moving exhibition in SoHo.

Most of all, there were those heart-breaking walls full of portraits that sprang up around the city, portraits of the missing who were later pronounced dead—the photography of desperate hope and finally of desperation. Once those portraits had been graduation and wedding pictures, family snapshots and publicity shots. The photographs in this book used to be aesthetic essays and urban art. They still are. But on September 11 they also became the saddest and some of the loveliest pictures of glory in the world.   *Vicki Goldberg, October 2001*

HARRY WILKS

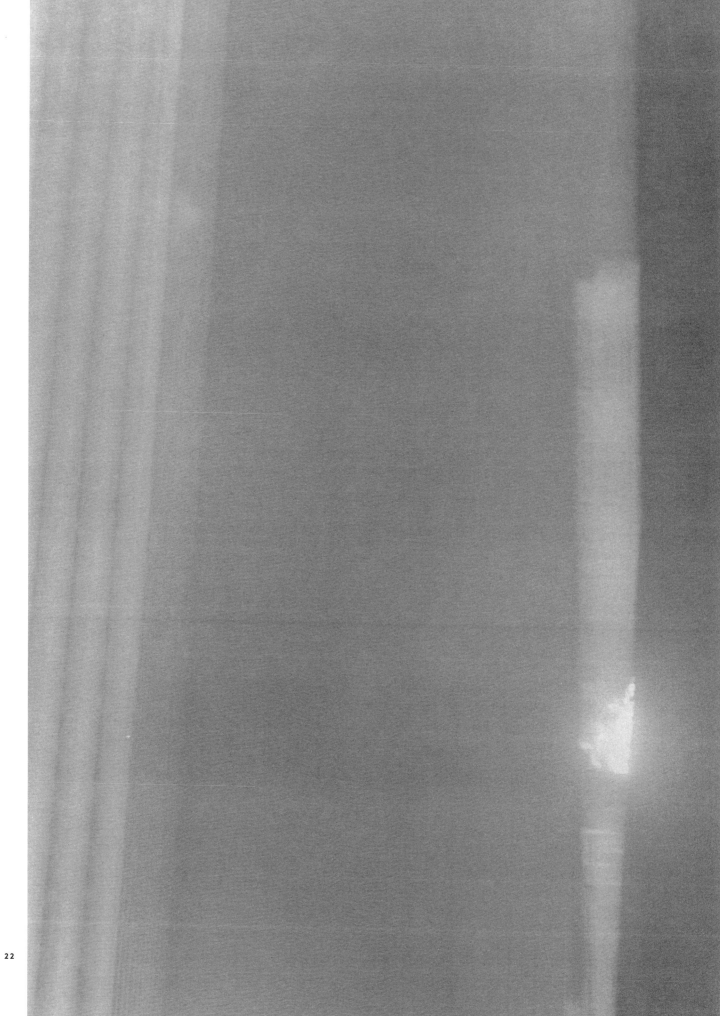

(ABOVE) **JOEL MEYEROWITZ**

(LEFT) **JOHN BERENS**

TOM BARIL

All proceeds from this book will be donated to the Shainwald Charitable Foundation
which will distribute monies to the humanitarian organizations Amnesty
International and Médecins Sans Frontières (Doctors Without Borders).

The publishers would like to thank all those who have made this project possible,
including all the photographers, Magnum Photos, and Getty Images for donating the
images, The Stinehour Press for printing, and Louise Fili Ltd for graphic design.

Printed by The Stinehour Press,
Lunenburg, Vermont